MILESTONES IN MODERN SCIENCE

The First Polio Vaccine

Guy de la Bédoyère

Gareth Stevens
Publishing

Please visit our web site at: www.garethstevens.com
For a free color catalog describing our list of high-quality books,
call 1-800-542-2595 (USA) or 1-800-387-3178 (Canada).
Our fax: (877) 542-2596.

Library of Congress Cataloging-in-Publication Data

De la Bédoyère, Guy.
    The first polio vaccine / by Guy de la Bédoyère.
       p. cm. — (Milestones in modern science)
    Includes bibliographical references and index.
    ISBN 0-8368-5855-7 (lib. bdg.)
    ISBN 0-8368-5862-X (softcover)
    1. Poliomyelitis vaccine—History—Juvenile literature. I. Title. II. Series.
  RA644.P9D4   2005
  614.5'49—dc22   2005040462

This North American edition first published in 2006 by
World Almanac® Library
An imprint of Gareth Stevens Publishing
1 Reader's Digest Road
Pleasantville, NY 10570-7000 USA

This edition copyright © 2006 by World Almanac® Library. First published by Evans Brothers Limited. Copyright © 2005 by Evans
Brothers Limited, 2A Portman Mansions, Chiltern Street, London W1U 6NR, United Kingdom. This U.S. edition published under
license from Evans Brothers Limited.

Evans Brothers Consultant: Dr. Anne Whitehead
Evans Brothers Editor: Sonya Newland
Evans Brothers Designer: D. R. Ink, info@d-r-ink.com
Evans Brothers Picture researcher: Julia Bird

World Almanac® Library editor: Carol Ryback
World Almanac® Library cover design and art direction: Tammy West

Photo credits: (t) top, (b) bottom, (r) right, (l) left
Science Photo Library: /7, 8(t), 9(b), 19(t); /National Library of Medicine cover, 11, 24(t), 26, 29(t), 35(t); /James King-Holmes cover, 21;
/Jean-Loup Charmet 6, 10, 12(b); /Stanley B. Burns, MD & the Burns Archive N.Y. 8(b), 18, 19(b), 28; /St. Bartholomew's Hospital 9(t);
/Sheila Terry 13(b); /Biphoto Associates 14; /Custom Medical Stock Photo 25(t), /CDC 25(b), 36(background); /S. Nagendra 40; /Russell
Kightley 41(r); /Saturn Stills 37; /Lowell Georgia 42; /Chris Priest & Mark Clarke 43(l). Science & Society Picture Library: /Science
Museum cover, 5, 12(t), 13(t), 17, 38(b); /National Museum of Photography, Film & Television/Daily Herald Archive 4(b); /Health
Education Authority 43(r). CORBIS: /© Bettmann 3, 20, 23(l), 29(b), 30, 31, 32, 33, 34, 36(inset); /© Rafiqur Rahman/Reuters 38(t); /
© Steve Raymer 41(l). TopFoto.co.uk: 4(t), 22, 23(b), 27, 44.

Printed in the United States of America

2 3 4 5 6 7 8 9 09 08

CONTENTS

ENTRANCE

for polio shots

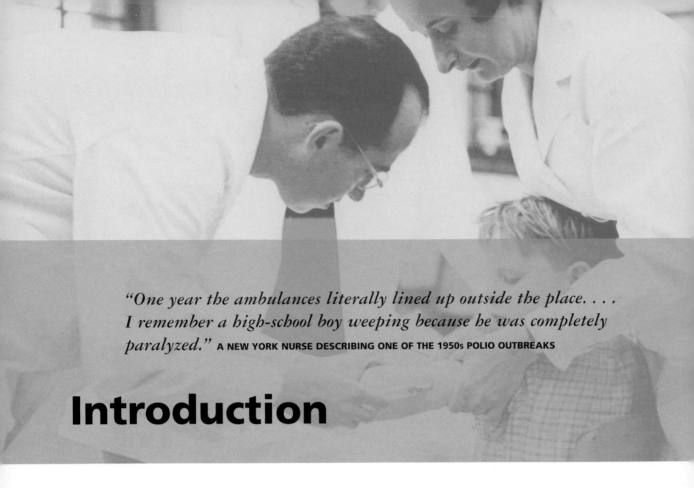

"One year the ambulances literally lined up outside the place. . . . I remember a high-school boy weeping because he was completely paralyzed." **A NEW YORK NURSE DESCRIBING ONE OF THE 1950s POLIO OUTBREAKS**

Introduction

Above: *Doctor Jonas Salk injects a young boy with a dose of polio vaccine in 1957.*

Below: *Polio can paralyze the chest muscles. In 1938, the only way to treat this condition was to use an "iron lung," a machine that helped polio sufferers breathe.*

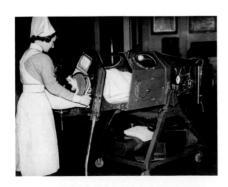

Polio is a terrible disease that can paralyze limbs, cause brain damage, and, in extreme cases, result in death. In the early to mid-twentieth century, polio epidemics ravaged developed countries, such as the United States, striking fear and causing widespread panic. Nobody knew what caused polio or how it spread. There were no effective treatments for the disease, and there was certainly no cure. Although many people recovered, many suffered the aftereffects of polio for the rest of their lives. Many ended up paralyzed or blinded. Doctors and scientists needed to find some way of preventing the disease.

Doctor Edward Jenner had created a smallpox vaccine in the late eighteenth century. Since that time, medical personnel knew that in some cases, exposing people to very small doses of a virus could result in immunity from the disease it caused. The dose of virus given by a vaccination was not concentrated enough to create a full-blown case of the disease, but it was enough for the body to react. People who received a vaccination created antibodies against the virus.

Could doctors prevent polio using a similar vaccination?

New polio cases reached a crisis point in the United States in the late 1930s. President Franklin D. Roosevelt established the National Foundation for Infantile Paralysis in 1938 to raise research funds to develop a polio vaccine. Aware of the need for preventative measures and gripped by a strong fear of contracting polio, people responded by sending generous donations. They turned to Dr. Jonas Salk to lead the research.

Salk soon discovered that the polio virus attacked in several different forms. Salk's research team faced a daunting task: Develop an effective technique to inactivate all three variations of the virus. Public pressure for a vaccine remained high. Despite the difficulties, the team created a vaccine with remarkable speed. Salk became as a hero as the country celebrated. The story didn't end there, however. More hurdles in polio prevention and treatment arose, and other scientists, including Albert Sabin, worked on improved and more effective vaccines against the disease. Sabin disagreed with the methods and vaccine produced by Salk.

Disagreements continue today about who developed the more effective polio vaccine: Sabin or Salk. At times, each technique was favored over the other as the preferred method of inoculation and prevention. Although Salk is remembered as the man who brought the disease under control, the contribution of other scientists, especially Sabin, cannot be underestimated. Thanks to the dedication and perseverance of these researchers, we enjoy a present level of polio prevention that was impossible only fifty years ago. Best of all, we stand on the brink of a polio-free world.

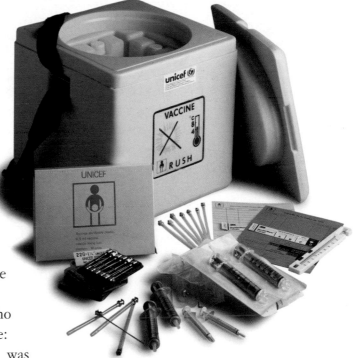

Above: Kits like this enable health organizations to establish worldwide vaccination programs that may help eliminate polio altogether in the next few years.

CHAPTER ONE

"I hope that one day the practice of producing cowpox in human beings will spread over the world—when that day comes, there will be no more smallpox." **EDWARD JENNER, c. 1798**

Early Experiments with Vaccines

Above: *Workers collect plague victims for burial. Plague became the most feared disease across Europe in the seventeenth century. At the time, people were unaware that fleas living on rats carried the plague-causing organism, which was passed to humans through flea bites. The disease spread quickly throughout the population and thousands of people died.*

For thousands of years, humans have tried to combat disease and infection. Unfortunately, without understanding the cause, treatment was largely guesswork and often ineffective. More important, preventing disease proved nearly impossible. This began to change in the seventeenth century, when severe outbreaks of diseases such as plague, cholera, and smallpox forced doctors and researchers to develop new methods of prevention.

TRADITIONAL MEDICINE

For many centuries, treatments for disease were based on observation and folklore. This was not as primitive as it sounds. Doctors in ancient Egypt and during the time of the Roman Empire treated patients for many types of illnesses. Surgery for wounds received in battle, chariot races, and gladiatorial fights was highly developed for its time. In spite of all this, infections continued to perplex physicians. They did not understand why diseases such as cholera and plague

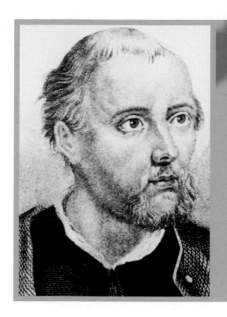

Key People

Paracelsus (*c.* 1493–1541) was a Swiss physician who pioneered alchemy in medicine. Alchemy was the search for hidden powers in substances that would bring health and prosperity. It was based on the idea that materials with similar properties or similar effects had a powerful, almost magical, relationship. Although some of his ideas seem strange to us now, Paracelsus's theories were advanced for their time. He challenged the belief that Greek and Roman medical writings were always correct. He suggested the use of specific remedies for specific diseases. For example, Paracelsus used mercury to treat syphilis. He also used opium as a medicine because it relieved pain.

occurred and spread so rapidly. The ancient Roman scholar Marcus Terrentius Varro (116–27 B.C.) speculated that minute animals in water caused malaria, but he could not prove this theory. The mystery surrounding the occurrence and spread of disease lasted for centuries.

In the 1600s, doctors still understood little about what caused plague and smallpox, two of the deadliest diseases at this time. Outbreaks of plague occurred across Europe. No treatment existed. In London in 1665, one hundred thousand people—about 25 percent of the population—died in the last major outbreak of plague. Smallpox also commonly affected people of all economic classes. No one knew how smallpox spread or how to prevent it. Queen Mary II, joint ruler of Britain with her husband, King William III, died of the disease when she was only thirty-two years old.

NEW SCIENCE

By this time, scientific thought was changing. The invention of the microscope in 1609 opened up a new world of discovery. It enabled people to see things not previously visible to the naked eye. Scientists exchanged new ideas instead of relying on Greek and Roman books. Investigating the causes of disease

Fact

SMALLPOX
After an incubation period of twelve days, victims of smallpox experienced headaches, high fevers, and back and limb pain, followed by skin eruptions three days later. Many victims survived with bad scars, but others were blinded, and many died. Although the last smallpox outbreak occurred in the late 1970s, copies of the deadly virus remain in secure laboratories. In 1980, the World Health Organization (WHO) announced the eradication of smallpox.

Key People

Samuel Hahnemann (1755–1843) was a German doctor greatly influenced by the works of Paracelsus (*see* p. 7). Frustrated by the medical practices of his time, Hahnemann began investigating different diseases and possible treatments. He found that the drug quinine seemed to cure malaria, an illness that caused a high fever, shaking, and headaches, but he also noticed that the drug itself actually caused symptoms similar to those of disease. Hahnemann called this his "Law of Similars," a principle that had its origins in alchemy. Quinine marked the first successful use of a chemical compound against an infectious disease.

Below: Doctors perform a vaccination experiment on a cow in the nineteenth century. Cowpox was similar to smallpox. Edward Jenner showed that humans infected with cowpox—a mild disease—gained immunity to the more dangerous smallpox.

became the driving force behind the new science of microscopic study.

In the 1700s, travelers from Turkey brought back news to Britain and the American colonies regarding smallpox. Turkish doctors rubbed fluid from smallpox pustules into skin cuts on unaffected patients to prevent

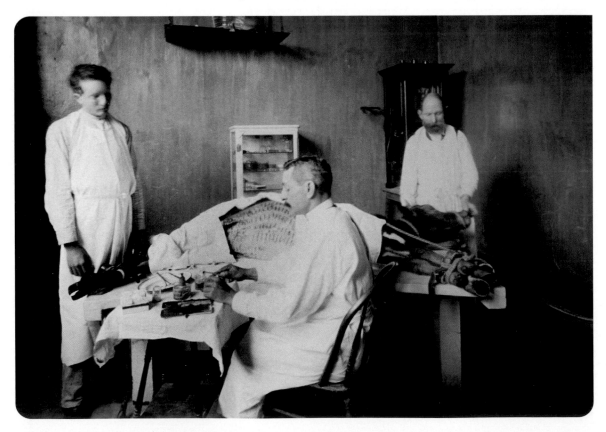

AN

INQUIRY

INTO

THE CAUSES AND EFFECTS

OF

THE VARIOLÆ VACCINÆ,

A DISEASE

DISCOVERED IN SOME OF THE WESTERN COUNTIES OF ENGLAND,

PARTICULARLY

GLOUCESTERSHIRE,

AND KNOWN BY THE NAME OF

THE COW POX.

BY EDWARD JENNER, M.D. F.R.S. &c.

——— QUID NOBIS CERTIUS IPSIS
SENSIBUS ESSE POTEST, QUO VERA AC FALSA NOTEMUS.
LUCRETIUS.

London:

PRINTED, FOR THE AUTHOR,

BY SAMPSON LOW, Nº. 7, BERWICK STREET, SOHO:

AND SOLD BY LAW, AVE-MARIA LANE; AND MURRAY AND HIGHLEY, FLEET STREET.

Left: Jenner published the results of his findings about cowpox in 1798. In the course of his experiments, some patients still became infected with smallpox. This was enough for scientists to scorn Jenner's beliefs about vaccination.

Below: Lady Mary Wortley Montagu had lived in Turkey, where they used a method of inoculation called variolation. People were injected with a dose of smallpox. In many instances, it prevented the full-blown disease from taking hold. Lady Mary introduced the practice to England on her return. It had a measure of success, although it was still risky.

the disease. This practice was called variolation, meaning "to infect with smallpox." In 1718, Lady Mary Wortley Montagu (1689–1762), the wife of the British ambassador in Constantinople, Turkey, introduced the practice on her return to England. At first, of course, people were wary of trying out this new method, so the technique was practiced on prisoners to see if it worked. The trials were successful and variolation became common in high society; even members of the British royal family were inoculated. Variolation was not an ideal solution, however, because there was always a chance a patient could catch full-blown smallpox.

THE GREAT COWPOX DISCOVERY

Edward Jenner became interested in the practice of variolation. He read about Hahnemann's studies and the "Law of Similars," in which treatments for diseases caused similar—although much milder—

Key People

Edward Jenner (1749–1823) had worked as an army doctor and then became a country doctor in Gloucestershire, England. In May 1796, a milkmaid called Sarah Nelmes came to see him. Sarah had a cowpox rash on her hand. Jenner saw his chance to prove that cowpox could immunize against smallpox. He made some scratches on the hand of his gardener's eight-year-old son, James Phipps. He rubbed into them some material he had scraped from Sarah's rash. James became ill with cowpox but soon recovered. From this, Jenner knew that cowpox could pass between human beings. Next he needed to prove that having cowpox would protect against smallpox. In July, Jenner deliberately infected James with smallpox. To the doctor's delight, James did not catch smallpox. Jenner finally had his proof.

Fact

DIPHTHERIA

In 1883, Theodor Klebs identified the bacterium that caused diphtheria, an acute infection of the throat. In the nineteenth and early twentieth centuries, diphtheria was common. It killed 10 percent of its victims. By 1888, researchers discovered that diphtheria bacteria produce a toxin. An antitoxin was discovered in 1891, but a reliable vaccine—a mixture of toxin and antitoxin—was not available until the 1920s. Researchers inactivated, or "killed," the toxin with a diluted formaldehyde solution known as formalin.

The principle of using an inactivated toxin played a major part in the struggle to find a polio vaccine.

symptoms to the diseases they prevented. Jenner began using Hahnemann's methods of documenting particular patient cases by keeping detailed notes on everything he saw.

Jenner noticed that the symptoms of smallpox resembled those of cowpox, a less dangerous, and not life-threatening, disease. Cowpox affected the udders of cows and sometimes transferred to humans who milked cows. One of the most significant findings that Jenner encountered was that people who caught cowpox did not catch smallpox. This observation proved to be a turning point in medical history— Jenner had hit on a way of protecting people from smallpox that was much safer than variolation. He began conducting practical experiments. In 1796, he proved that deliberately infecting someone with cowpox made them immune to smallpox.

Jenner published his results in 1798, but progress was slow. Since no one yet understood how the disease spread, and standards of hygiene were low, the samples of cowpox being used for the immunization became contaminated with smallpox virus. As a result, several of Jenner's patients came down with the deadly disease and some died. This cast doubts upon the process.

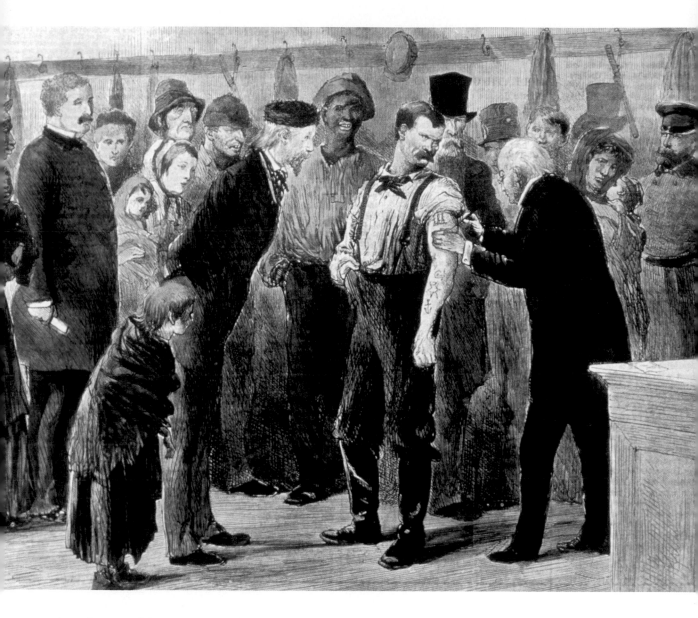

Another problem was that doctors who practiced variolation became jealous of Jenner's discovery and did not want to lose patients and money to the new technique. These doctors ridiculed Jenner and mocked his methods. Political cartoons showed people with cows' heads. Jenner knew he had made a great discovery, however, and persisted with his trials. His perseverance paid off. Eventually, researchers reluctantly admitted that Jenner's method of inoculation proved safer than variolation. In 1853, thirty years after his death, England passed a law

Above: At first, the public greeted Jenner's vaccine with contempt, but within a few years people realized its effectiveness and it became compulsory. This 1873 engraving shows working-class people in England lined up to receive the vaccine.

making Jenner's method for preventing smallpox compulsory. The technique was called "vaccination," from the Latin word for cowpox: *Vaccinia*.

NEW RESEARCH INTO DISEASE

Now that Jenner had proved the idea of preventing a disease by infecting people with a less dangerous but similar disease, doctors and scientists started looking for the same solution for other diseases. Many advances occurred in science around this time, and people's understanding of the world around them also expanded. French scientist Louis Pasteur made one of the most important discoveries. Pasteur studied diseases that affected animals, including anthrax, chicken cholera, and rabies. He wondered if something in the air carried the diseases and passed them from one animal to another. To test his theory,

Above: *This gauge from the 1920s was used to measure the size of smallpox pustules. Doctors related the pustules to four different sizes, which indicated the stage of the disease—the larger the pustules, the more progressed the disease.*

Right: *French scientist Louis Pasteur conducted experiments on the fermentation of beer and wine in his laboratory.*

Pasteur conducted experiments with liquids, first storing them in airtight containers, and then storing them in open-air containers. His experiments proved that airborne microorganisms caused disease and decay. Scientists previously believed that microorganisms were a by-product of decay. From this point on, researchers made great advances in identifying the different bacteria that caused different diseases. The fact that scientists could cultivate, grow, and observe the behavior of bacteria under a microscope increased the progress and occurrence of scientific advancements. One of the key discoveries was that scientists finally realized how rapidly bacteria could multiply.

Despite these advances, scientists found that even when all the bacteria and other visible microorganisms were filtered out, some diseases and infections still occurred. In 1898, an experiment showed that foot-and-mouth, a disease that affected hoofed animals, could still infect another animal even when everything visible had been filtered out. From this they concluded that there must be something else causing foot-and-mouth and other diseases, that survived the filtration process. Such infections were called filter-passing viruses. No one saw these tiny viruses until the powerful electron microscope was invented in 1937.

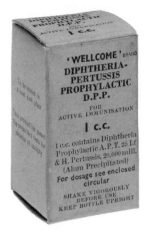
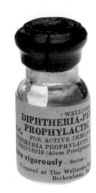

Above: Jenner's work on vaccines opened up a new field of research. In the 1920s, an effective vaccine for diphtheria was produced. This killed-virus vaccine influenced the development of the polio vaccine just a few years later.

Key People

Louis Pasteur (1822–1895) was a French scientist whose experiments were a turning point in the understanding of the causes of disease. To learn what made certain substances decay, he took different liquids—wine, beer, and milk—and placed them in special sealed containers so that airborne microorganisms could not get in. The beer and wine did not ferment and the milk did not get sour. When he left containers of those liquids open to the air for a few days, allowing the microorganisms to affect the contents, the milk went sour and the wine and beer started to ferment. Until Pasteur's work, many scientists believed that microorganisms grew only when substances rotted. Pasteur's experiments proved that microorganisms were everywhere, all the time, and could cause disease and decay.

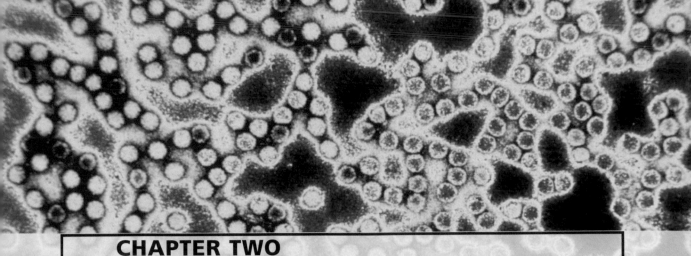

CHAPTER TWO

"There were polio epidemics all the time. You wouldn't go out and play. You wouldn't go to a county fair, wouldn't go to a public swimming location." BEN WECHSLER, A PENNSYLVANIA SCHOOLBOY

The Polio Virus

Above: *This electron micrograph shows a collection of the viruses that cause polio. Polioviruses are very tiny— approximately 25 nanometers (billionths of a meter) in diameter.*

The disease poliomyelitis has been around for many centuries, but in the middle of the nineteenth century, it began to appear in a much more severe form. Previously, many people acquired immunity to polio through weakened strains of the disease that were transmitted, for example, through poor sanitation (*see* p. 18). As hygiene standards improved, fewer people were exposed to the weakened strains of the virus. Instead, full-blown cases of polio erupted. Thousands of children became permanently crippled in polio outbreaks. Widespread panic occurred because no one knew how to prevent or cure the disease.

WHAT IS A VIRUS?

A virus is a microorganism made of nucleic acid. It is visible only under a powerful electron microscope. Two thousand of the largest viruses lined up side by side would measure just 0.039 inch (1 millimeter) in length. Viruses differ from bacteria, the microorganisms that cause diseases such as typhoid fever and diphtheria. Bacteria are single-celled organisms that can live on their own. They have their own DNA (deoxyribonucleic acid), which contains the genetic instructions for life and allows them to grow and reproduce without help from another organism.

Unlike bacteria, viruses are parasites and cannot live on their own. Viruses do not have their own DNA. Instead, they have only RNA (ribonucleic acid). Different types of virus attack different cells—for example, the flu virus attacks cells in the digestive tract, and the HIV virus attacks cells in the immune system. Most types of virus work in the same way, however. They attach themselves to the cells and then steal resources that their RNA needs to reproduce. When that happens, the host cell can no longer do its own job properly.

All organisms, including bacteria and viruses, carry proteins on their surface that have a unique "chemical fingerprint" called an antigen. When invading

Below: How a vaccine works: A weakened form of the virus is injected into the blood. Immune cells in the body create antibodies that kill the weakened virus. If the virus enters that body in the future, the antibodies recognize and kill the invading virus.

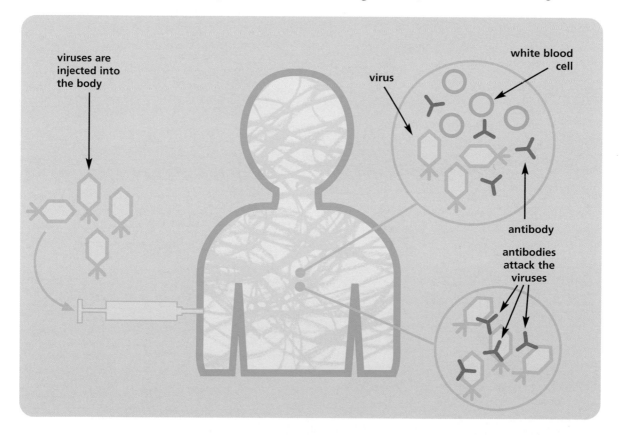

viruses are injected into the body

virus

white blood cell

antibody

antibodies attack the viruses

bacteria or viruses enter a body, their antigens trigger reactions in the host's immune system. Millions of white blood cells (WBCs) in the host's body recognize individual antigens and make antibodies to fight off invaders. The immune system "remembers" each antigen, and if that virus or bacteria ever enters the body again, the WBCs are ready with antibodies. Acquired immunity occurs when someone has had a disease and developed antibodies to it. Normally, it takes several days for WBCs to make new antibodies to attack a new enemy, and sometimes this does not happen in time to stop a disease from harming the victim. A vaccine uses low doses, which cause the body to make antibodies without

Fact

BACTERIA AND VIRUSES

Bacteria and viruses are the most common causes of disease. People often confuse the two, although they are quite different. Bacteria possess the ability to reproduce on their own. Viruses must invade living cells in order to reproduce and cause disease. A group of drugs known as antibiotics can treat bacteria, either by killing the microorganisms in the body or preventing their growth or reproduction. Antibiotics do not work against viruses because viruses are not cells and do not feed or reproduce the same way as bacteria. When the body's immune system kills a virus, it must kill the entire cell in which the virus lives.

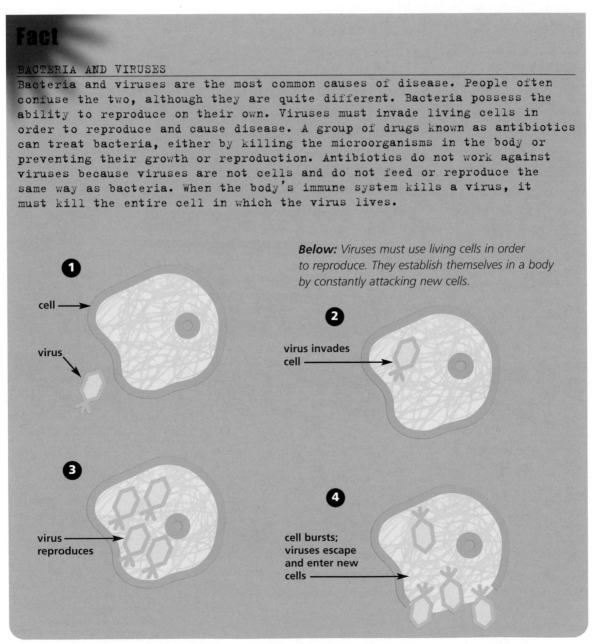

Below: Viruses must use living cells in order to reproduce. They establish themselves in a body by constantly attacking new cells.

1

cell →

virus

2

virus invades cell →

3

virus reproduces →

4

cell bursts; viruses escape and enter new cells →

allowing the disease to develop into a dangerous form. Booster vaccinations are sometimes needed to keep antibody levels high enough to fight diseases.

Viruses cannot live on their own, so in order to breed them for study and vaccine use, they must be grown on living tissue. This proved a major problem in developing the polio vaccine.

POLIO—THE DISEASE

Poliomyelitis is very infectious. The virus that causes it, poliovirus, gets into the body through the mouth and finds its way to the intestine, where it reproduces. It passes easily out of the body in feces. If the virus gets into the water supply in places with poor sanitation, it can infect large segments of a population.

Many people who catch polio have no symptoms. They have no idea they carry the disease and are infectious to other people. This makes polio very

Above: Polio can cause paralysis of the chest muscles. Some victims needed an artificial respirator to breathe. During the outbreaks in the first half of the twentieth century, "iron lungs" helped people breathe. An iron lung was almost the length of a car. It exerted a "push-pull" effect on the sufferer's chest to force air in and out of his or her lungs. An iron lung kept the polio victim breathing until he or she recovered enough muscle function to breathe without assistance. Some people spent years or even decades living in an iron lung. In fact, some people still breathe using an iron lung today—even though newer technology exists.

Fact

SYMPTOMS OF POLIO
Polio victims who catch
the disease feel fine for
a week or two, but may
experience a fever and
a headache. Most get no
worse and soon recover;
for the rest, the
symptoms begin again
after a week. Their necks
get stiff and the tissues
surrounding the brain and
spinal cord become
irritated. If patients
do not recover within a
month, the damage is
usually permanent and
they are left paralyzed.

Above: *With the help of crutches and a therapist, this little boy worked to rebuild strength in his legs. Some polio victims recover completely, but others are left with weakened limbs.*

difficult to contain. Sometimes the poliovirus moves from the intestine and into the nervous system, where it does much most harm by causing paralysis.

One in two hundred polio victims becomes permanently paralyzed; as many as 10 percent or more may die unless they are put in an artificial respirator because their chest muscles no longer work well enough for them to breathe. There is no cure for polio. It can attack anyone, at any age. Children are more likely to be affected than adults, however.

Although some people living in Egypt more than three thousand years ago may have become paralyzed by poliovirus, at that time—and for many centuries afterward—the disease rarely caused serious harm. It was so common that babies under six months old often caught polio but were saved by antibodies passed on from their mothers in breast milk, which gave them time to develop their own antibodies against the disease. Very few children became ill, but those that did and became paralyzed were usually under three years old. Mostly, these victims would walk with a limp or have a withered arm where paralysis had caused the muscles to waste.

In the nineteenth century, polio became a serious problem. Dirty streets and open sewers running through cities allowed human feces carrying poliovirus to contaminate the water supplies. Still, people did not realize that this is what caused the spread of the disease. Polio could break out almost anywhere at anytime. The first recorded outbreak was in Nottinghamshire, England, in 1835. Another probable outbreak occurred in the United States, in Louisiana in 1841. Reports of polio increased in many other places during that time, especially in the Scandinavian countries. Things soon became worse: Paralysis caused by polio not only affected more people, but also caused those who contracted it to experience a more severe form of paralysis than ever before.

Key People

Karl Landsteiner (1868–1943) was one of the first doctors to investigate the possibility of a polio vaccine. In 1909, he gave polio to monkeys by injecting them with tissue taken from a deceased human polio victim. In this way, he showed that an infectious virus was the cause of the disease. Early attempts to find a vaccine proved frustrating because no one knew there were three different types of poliovirus: A vaccine that worked against one type of poliovirus was useless against the other two. In 1931, scientists realized that more than one poliovirus type caused the disease. In 1948, researchers finally confirmed that there were three main types of poliovirus.

THE POLIO CRISIS

In 1907, a polio breakout in New York City, affected more than two thousand people. In 1916, a polio epidemic affected nearly thirty thousand people across twenty states. More than seven thousand died. In New York City alone, nine thousand were affected and about twenty-five hundred died. After that, serious outbreaks occurred nearly every summer. More older children, teenagers, and adults caught the disease.

Fact

PHARAOH SIPTAH
In 1898, the mummy of the Egyptian pharaoh Siptah, who died in 1198 B.C., was found. His left leg was withered and shorter than the right one. The pharaoh probably caught polio in early life and must have walked with very great difficulty.

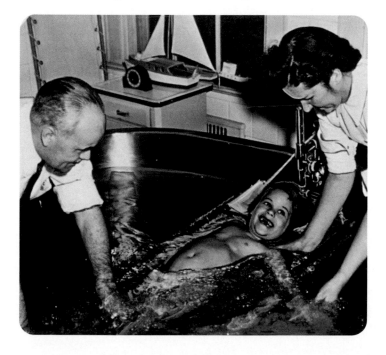

Left: *A young polio patient smiles as she is immersed in a tub of swirling water as part of her treatment. Doctors used water therapy to rebuild muscles that had been wasted by the disease, but many victims remained paralyzed.*

Below: *During the 1916 polio outbreak in New York City, people were so afraid of the disease that they fled the city by the thousands.*

Why did polio suddenly become so much more widespread and more severe? It was possibly the result of the way people's everyday lives had changed. By the early twentieth century, fewer mothers were breast-feeding their babies, so fewer children received the polio antibodies they needed to fight the disease. Although sanitation levels had improved, polio could still pass between people where they gathered, especially in swimming pools, where water was easily contaminated. Young people often had no antibodies to fight the disease and were more likely to become paralyzed if they caught the virus.

Between 1916 and 1934, more than 50 percent of reported polio cases in the world occurred in the United States and Canada, causing widespread terror. The sight of paralyzed children and young people

Fact

THE INFLUENZA EPIDEMIC

In 1918, a severe form of influenza broke out. As the virus spread across the United States and Europe, it killed millions. Medical experts reasoned that dietary restrictions that occurred because of WWI had left many peoples' immune systems susceptible to disease. In the U.S., 25 million people caught influenza and about half a million died. It was the worst epidemic in history until HIV/AIDS became widespread in the 1980s.

Right: Tissue samples from victims of the influenza epidemic of 1918 are spread across a list of those who died.

horrified the public. Many victims caught polio after being in public places, so hospitals were afraid of caring for those with the disease. Many people panicked and fled from the cities, while "con men" started a thriving trade in so-called "miracle cures."

After the 1916 epidemic, the U.S. Public Health Service realized that most of New York City's population had probably caught polio, but because they did not become ill, they had no idea they were carrying or spreading the disease. This meant that putting victims in quarantine would not work—too many people were likely carrying the disease. Only a vaccine could protect everyone.

In 1934, public fund-raising began to help finance the search for a vaccine. More than $1 million was raised immediately. Although the problem of

THE MARCH OF DIMES
The U.S. campaign to raise money for polio research was known as "The March of Dimes," because it urged people to show their support for the cause by sending their dimes directly to the President. In 1938, Americans sent $268,000 in dimes to the National Foundation for Infantile Paralysis. About $1.8 million was raised that year in total. In 1955, nearly $67 million was spent on polio patient care, information, education, and further research into the devastating disease.

Right: Prince Rainier III of Monaco and his wife, actress Grace Kelly, promoted the fund-raising effort known as the March of Dimes.

financing was being addressed, other scientific issues also needed resolving. Most important, no one knew how to measure poliovirus or the antibodies it produced. Until this was possible, coming up with a correct dosage of the vaccine was pretty much impossible. Also, researchers still could not distinguish one type of poliovirus from another.

These facts did not prevent some scientists from rushing ahead and vaccinating children without thorough testing. Dr. John Kolmer of Temple University Medical School in Philadelphia, Pennsylvania, created a vaccine from a poliovirus that he believed was harmless. He vaccinated twelve thousand children before testing it properly. Six of the children died and three became paralyzed. Such disasters made other scientists doubt the chances of the development of a reliable polio vaccine.

THE NATIONAL FOUNDATION FOR INFANTILE PARALYSIS

In 1938, U.S. president Franklin D. Roosevelt established the National Foundation for Infantile Paralysis (NFIP). Roosevelt himself suffered from paralysis that, at the time, was believed to have been caused by polio. He caught the disease in 1921, when he was nearly forty years old. He wore steel braces on his legs and found it very difficult to walk, so he spent much of his time in a wheelchair. Although he downplayed his disability in public, he used his position as president to promote research into the disease. Before he founded the NFIP, he organized and hosted many fund-raising events. In 2003, researchers suggested that Roosevelt may not have had polio after all, but instead may have suffered from a disease called Guillain-Barré Syndrome, which causes the immune system to attack healthy tissue, resulting in many symptoms similar to those of polio. At the time, no effective treatments for either disease existed. Today, the cause of Guillain-Barré Syndrome remains a puzzle. Most patients now recover from the disease, but often spend months in an intensive care unit. Many end up confined to a wheelchair.

Roosevelt's National Foundation was a great success. Supported by public donations, the NFIP became known as "The March of Dimes" after urging people to donate their dimes to the cause. The organization searched for a researcher who could develop a vaccine for them. That man was Jonas Salk.

ABOVE: *U.S. president Franklin D. Roosevelt walks with the help of crutches in 1928. He established the National Foundation for Infantile Paralysis (NFIP) in 1938 to raise money for research into a vaccine. The NFIP later became known as "The March of Dimes."*

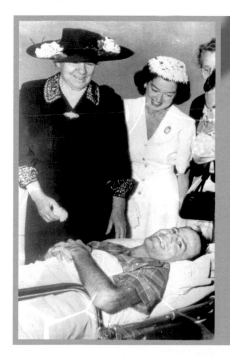

Key People

Sister Elizabeth Kenny (1880–1952, pictured on the left) was an Australian nurse who became well-known in the 1930s and 1940s for her treatment of polio victims. Polio victims who became paralyzed were usually placed in plaster casts in the belief that the extra support would prevent their limbs from becoming deformed. Other victims wore heavy leg irons and braces that seriously limited movement and recovery. Sister Kenny believed treatment with moist hot packs on muscles, when combined with exercise and retraining of muscle movement, helped patients recover the use of their limbs. At a time when there was no polio vaccine, Sister Kenny had considerable success and became famous in Australia, Britain, and the United States. Her love of publicity and lack of scientific expertise made her unpopular with some doctors, but her instinctive knowledge made a real difference to the lives of many polio victims.

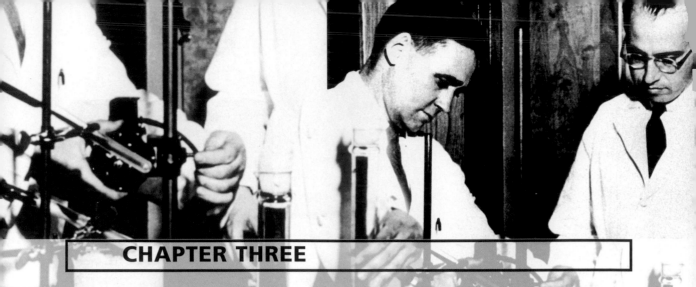

CHAPTER THREE

"It is courage based on confidence, not daring, and it is confidence based on experience."

JONAS SALK, ON TRYING THE EXPERIMENTAL VACCINE ON HIMSELF AND HIS FAMILY

Salk's Investigations

D r. Jonas Salk had a special interest in vaccines. He joined the research team led by Dr. Thomas Francis at the University of Michigan in Ann Arbor. Under Francis, Salk helped search for an influenza vaccine. He succeeded in developing one for use during World War II. The U.S. Army, which feared an outbreak of influenza as serious as that of 1918–1919, sponsored the research. Salk's work was vital to the development of vaccines to control viruses. In 1947, the University of Pittsburgh's School of Medicine in Pennsylvania hired him to continue his work on influenza. This lucky combination of sites and personalities played out well in medical history.

Above: Dr. Jonas Salk (right), conducted experiments to discover a vaccine to combat the three types of poliovirus.

SALK'S SOLUTIONS

Harry Weaver, a leading member of the National Foundation for Infantile Paralysis, paid a visit to Salk at Pittsburgh, asking him to head the polio vaccine research funded by President Roosevelt's organization. Salk was delighted at the opportunity: The search for a polio vaccine was a high-profile, national campaign that would make available the money and resources Salk needed to hire the right team. If it proved successful, the arrangement offered Salk the chance to develop an important medical treatment that would

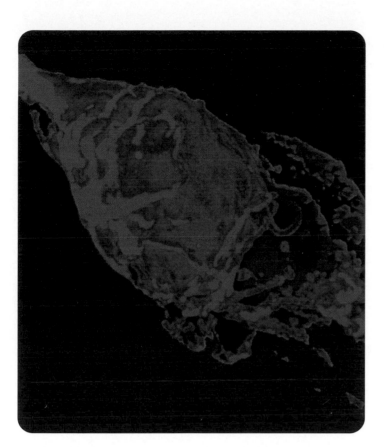

Above: *A cell infected with poliovirus magnified 9,000 times. The red patches at center right are poliovirus microorganisms attacking the cell's surface.*

Fact

TYPES OF POLIOVIRUS
One of the major problems scientists found in creating a polio vaccine was that there are three different types of poliovirus. Vaccinating against one did not prevent a person from getting a different type. Modern vaccines include all three types of virus.

TYPE I: Most often causes epidemics; it frequently results in paralysis of the legs, arms and breathing muscles.

TYPE II: Least likely to cause paralysis, but infection can result in severe damage to the brain stem.

TYPE III: Rarest but also most dangerous; causes leg and arm paralysis as well as brain stem damage.

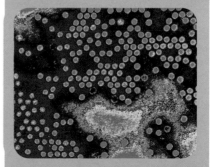

Above: *A poliovirus (green) belonging to Type I. Type I is the virus that causes most epidemics and often results in paralysis.*

be recognized not only across the United States, but also in many other countries—particularly across Europe—that suffered the effects of poliomyelitis.

By the time Salk set up his research team and started working on a polio vaccine, the need for a reliable treatment became even more urgent. Polio outbreaks occurred almost annually, and people were growing more and more afraid of this terrible disease.

Scientists already knew that 125 individual forms of polioviruses existed. The symptoms of the disease led them to believe that these could be divided into three "types," numbered I, II and III (*see* Fact box). A completely effective vaccine had to work against all three types; otherwise, a patient could easily catch another version of the viruses, even if vaccinated. Salk's goal involved determining to which of the three types

Fact

KILLED VIRUSES
Vaccines like the one used for smallpox are called "live-virus" vaccines. They contain small, living doses of the disease. The polio vaccine Jonas Salk developed was a "killed-virus" vaccine because the dosage of the virus that it contained was harmless. Later, Albert Sabin developed another "live-virus" version of the polio vaccine. Much of the current debate about which vaccine is most effective is based on whether scientists and doctors think that killed-virus vaccines or live-virus vaccines are better for the patient.

each of the 125 viruses belonged. It was an enormous task, and the established process of testing was slow and expensive. Salk decided to search for a more efficient way to find the answer.

Salk's solution was brilliant. He realized that although some polioviruses are much weaker than others, they all encourage the body to make similar numbers of antibodies. He gave a poliovirus of an unknown type to a monkey. The monkey developed antibodies, which Salk then tested against polioviruses of a known type. If the monkey's antibodies killed a Type I virus, then the unknown virus must be Type I. If not, the antibodies had to instead work against either Type II or Type III—so he next used those antibodies against a Type II poliovirus. If they killed the Type II virus, then Salk knew the unknown virus was also a Type II; if not, it had to be Type III. Scientists criticized Salk for changing the established methods of researching the vaccine. Most preferred tried-and-proved methods when it came to medical research, but Salk knew the need was desperate. His methods were much faster.

THE PACE OF RESEARCH QUICKENS

Two other polio researchers, working independently, helped Salk look for a safe vaccine. In 1948, Dr. Isabel Morgan of Baltimore, Maryland, grew the poliovirus antibodies in nervous tissue from the spinal cords of

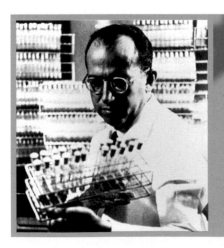

Key People

Jonas Salk (1914–1995) had planned to study law, but while at the City College of New York, he grew interested in biology and chemistry and especially the study of diseases. He went on to study at the New York University School of Medicine in Manhattan. Salk was interested in whether viruses such as influenza and polio could be made harmless but still be effective as a vaccine. He was convinced it would work, even though at the time nobody else believed it would. It turned out he was right. Salk's method became known as the "inactive" or "killed" virus method.

monkeys and then killed the poliovirus with formalin, thus creating polio antibodies in monkeys without infecting them with the disease. Although the monkey vaccine could not benefit humans, who are highly allergic to nervous tissue from other animals, her research was a step in the right direction.

Around the same time, another independent team made a great breakthrough. Bacterial infections had prevented previous researchers from growing viruses on scraps of living tissue. John F. Enders, Ph.D., working in Boston, Massachusetts, had successfully grown poliovirus in a test tube that contained nonnervous tissue from human embryos and monkeys. Ender's method used penicillin, the new antibiotic drug, to kill any bacterial infections on tissue cultures. Salk and his team used Ender's technique to grow as much poliovirus as needed for thorough study.

Above: John F. Enders (right) and Dr. Thomas Weller examine poliovirus in a tissue culture at their research laboratory in Boston, Massachusetts, in 1954. Enders' experiments in growing polioviruses on nonnervous tissue meant that Salk and his team could grow as much as they needed for their own investigations.

THE PRESSURE TO FIND A VACCINE
In 1952, there was a serious
polio outbreak in Copenhagen,
Denmark, and another in the
United States, where nearly
58,000 cases were reported
and more than 3,000 people
died. Once again, the nations
affected were thrown into panic
on a huge scale. Parents kept
children away from public places
and even schools, fearing that
the infection would strike their
families without warning. People
even avoided visiting each others'
houses for fear of catching the
disease. Such a disaster had a
positive effect, however. A public
outcry for a vaccine arose. In
the U.S., the country leading the
research, the government did not
struggle to find funding. The
situation was so serious that
everybody was willing to donate.

Above: *A man in an iron lung in an ambulance in the early 1950s. The mirror on the iron lung allowed the patient to see what was going on around him or her.*

THE SUCCESS OF THE MONKEY TRIALS

Salk divided his research team into groups, each working on a specific task. One team goal was to determine on which monkey tissue the polio grew best. Another team worked on making poliovirus inactive but still effective enough to produce antibodies when injected into laboratory animals.

In 1951, the researchers began injecting monkeys with poliovirus. Until Salk's work, many scientists thought that only live vaccines could cause the production of antibodies. Salk believed that an inactive virus vaccine would work just as well and more safely. He knew that formalin was already being used to make an inactive diphtheria virus vaccine, and he reasoned that this technique might also work on his own vaccine. Salk's team used formalin to inactivate the poliovirus. His team discovered that monkeys' kidney tissue provided the best medium for growing the virus from which the vaccine could be made.

Salk and his team worked quickly, but many issues remained: most vital was determining exactly how much formalin to use. Too much formalin in the vaccine could damage the virus so much that the patients would not produce antibodies when given the vaccine. Too little formalin might cause the patient to develop full-blown polio before his or her immune system could produce enough antibodies to fight it off.

Key People

Dr. Hilary Koprowski (b. 1916) was an industrial researcher and one of the pioneers of the polio vaccine. He began his research in 1947. Although Salk was still testing his vaccine on monkeys, Koprowski went one step further. In 1950, he conducted an unofficial experiment. He used a weakened Type II poliovirus to experiment on children. His experiment worked: The children developed antibodies and none got polio. Thanks to Koprowski, Salk knew that successful tests of vaccines on monkeys indicated that the vaccines should likely work on humans as well.

In 1952, Salk and his researchers hit on the right amount of formalin to make a vaccine against all three types of poliovirus. The vaccine was strong enough to encourage the production of antibodies against all forms of polio, yet too weak to be dangerous. It was called "inactive" polio vaccine, or IPV. The team spent a year testing it on monkeys. For greatest efficacy, the vaccine was given in two doses, one month apart. The researchers estimated that boosters would be needed after five years to maintain immunity.

While Salk and his team worked frantically to satisfy the public demand for a successful vaccine, the panic continued across Europe and the U.S. Salk knew they had to work fast. His luck held out. Trials showed that the IPV worked. The monkeys did not catch polio from the vaccine and developed antibodies to the virus. After three weeks, the monkeys did not catch polio even when deliberately infected. Human trials came next.

Background: A young girl turns away as Salk—helped by a nurse—gives a dose of his vaccine during the trials he began in 1952.

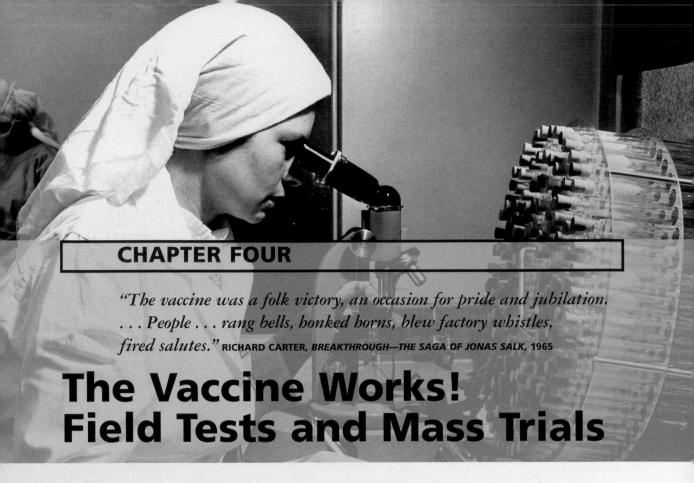

CHAPTER FOUR

*"The vaccine was a folk victory, an occasion for pride and jubilation.
. . . People . . . rang bells, honked horns, blew factory whistles,
fired salutes."* RICHARD CARTER, *BREAKTHROUGH—THE SAGA OF JONAS SALK*, 1965

The Vaccine Works!
Field Tests and Mass Trials

Above: A technician inspects samples of polio vaccine at a laboratory in California during the mass trials that took place throughout 1954.

Testing a new vaccine is risky. If it goes wrong, the vaccine can cause the disease it is supposed to prevent. Still, the polio vaccine had to be tested on people. Salk decided to try out his vaccine on patients who had already had polio because he knew they could not catch it again.

HUMAN TRIALS BEGIN

Salk started secret trials at a home for polio victims in Leetsdale, Pennsylvania, in June 1952. He took blood samples from forty-five children who had had polio and from twenty-seven staff members who had not had the disease. He wanted to see if the vaccine would raise antibody levels in both groups.

Salk found that the polio vaccine "boosted" the antibody levels in the children. It also gave the staff members the same level of antibodies they would have had following a natural infection. Salk placed the blood samples from the vaccinated people on tissue cultures of poliovirus. Antibodies in this blood killed the virus. The early signs were promising.

Although Salk used many volunteers, he needed to try it out on even more people. Trials of any new vaccine must be as extensive as possible to provide the greatest chance of detecting any side effects. Excitement grew when Salk published his early results, and mass trials of the vaccine began.

The mass trials started in the spring of 1954. The vaccine would be used in 217 areas in 44 states, with about 30,000 medical staff and others involved in managing the project. Around 1.8 million schoolchildren, between six and nine years old, received the vaccine. The program was one of the first in history to use computers for recording data. Every child's progress had to be monitored accurately.

A BAD BATCH

On April 12, 1955, the tenth anniversary of Franklin D. Roosevelt's death, Salk announced that the vaccine was effective. He became a national hero, something he feared, because he believed others would label him a "glory hound." Some of his medical rivals were indeed jealous, especially since journalists called his discovery the "Salk vaccine." Other critics labeled Salk's achievement a "quest for personal glory" that depended on the unacknowledged work of a lot of other researchers.

The general public did not care. They were ecstatic. The disease that for so long had cast a shadow of fear over their lives—a disease that caused disabilites in children

Left: *Just minutes after the success of the Salk vaccine was announced in 1955, officials load cases of the vaccine onto planes in Philadelphia, Pennsylvania, for distribution throughout the United States. Wyeth, a Philadelphia-based pharmaceutical company, manufactured and distributed the vaccine.*

Fact

MASS VACCINATIONS
By August 1955, more than four million vaccinations had been given. In the same year, about 30,000 cases of polio occurred in the United States. In 1956, it was half that, and by 1957, there were just 6,000 cases.

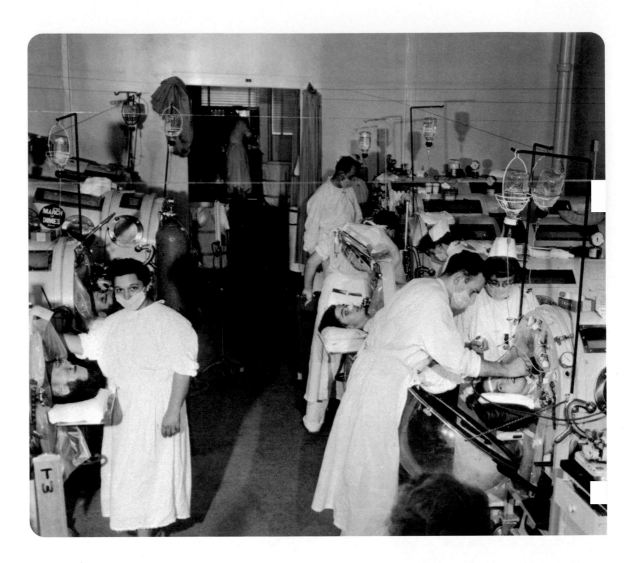

Above: *In 1955, the year Salk announced the success of the polio vaccine, the need for a vaccine had reached its peak. This hospital ward in Boston, Massachusetts, shows why: Many people were living in iron lungs to help them breathe, and cases of polio in the U.S. were widespread.*

Next page: *Samples of Salk's first vaccine from 1955. This box contains three vials of the vaccine made by Cutter Laboratories of Berkeley, California. Some vaccines made by Cutter caused polio to develop.*

and young people—finally appeared controllable. Word spread, and Salk's polio vaccine was rapidly introduced in countries around the world.

Despite the high hopes, concerns that a live virus might get into the vaccine had surfaced during the mass trials. Within a month of the release of the vaccine, some vaccinated children had caught polio. People were devastated. Immunization was immediately suspended and investigations into the new cases of polio were ordered. If true, it would destroy the principle behind Salk's inactive-virus vaccine.

Investigators traced the cases back to a bad batch of vaccine, made by Cutter Laboratories of Berkeley, California, that contained live poliovirus. About 260 cases of polio occurred in 25 states, and 11 people died. Idaho was probably the worst affected: 25 children caught polio from the vaccine and passed it on to 61 other people. Of the 86 involved in the Idaho outbreak, 70 were paralyzed.

Some experts wanted immunization stopped permanently. They charged that the vaccine batches were not properly tested, even though from the start researchers had made clear the risk of live viruses ending up in vaccines. Salk helped tighten production standards. Immunizations resumed, but Salk's opponents had the proof they wanted that an inactive vaccine was potentially unreliable. Some members of the public still feared children would catch polio from the vaccine. In New York City, up to 30 percent of the children did not show up for their immunizations.

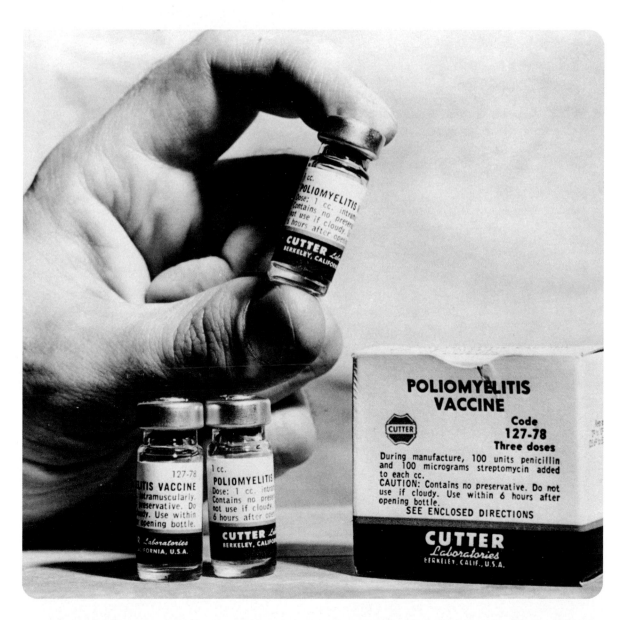

CHAPTER FIVE

"The Salk Vaccine is Safe, Effective, and Potent. Polio is Conquered."
U.S. NEWSPAPER HEADLINE, APRIL 12, 1955

New Vaccines

Above: *In 1955, thousands of schoolchildren, like these in San Diego, California, received the polio vaccine as part of a mass-inoculation program.*

Next page: *Between 1916 and 1934, the United States and Canada reported more than half of the cases of polio worldwide. After the outbreak in 1916 (occurring mainly in New York City), cases of polio declined and then leveled off—although the disease was still very much in evidence. The epidemic reached its peak in 1952. With the introduction of the vaccine, cases dropped dramatically, and by 1965, the United States reported only sixty-one new cases.*

Salk's new polio vaccine signaled a massive breakthrough, but was far from perfect. Although the public believed that Salk's polio vaccine was 100 percent effective, in reality, it was only about 90 percent effective. After the Cutter incident, many lost confidence in the safety of the vaccine. The vaccine was also expensive and difficult to produce. Vaccinating large numbers of people was time-consuming and costly. For the best efficacy, Salk's vaccine required two injections, with booster shots every five years for life.

SABIN VERSUS SALK

Even after the Salk vaccine proved effective, Dr. Albert Sabin, who was working on a different polio vaccine, attacked Salk in newspaper articles and interviews. Salk was also criticized by other scientists. The rivalry was partly responsible for Enders' team (instead of Salk) receiving the 1954 Nobel Prize for medicine for the discovery that viruses could be grown on ordinary living tissue without fear of contamination.

Key People

Albert Sabin (1906–1993) spent a lifetime researching vaccines and viral diseases, including polio. From 1939 until 1974, he worked at Ohio's University of Cincinnati College of Medicine. Sabin disproved the notion that poliovirus entered the body via the nose and instead entered through the mouth. He promoted the idea that children probably acquired polio antibodies through exposure to a weakened strain of poliovirus transferred via poor sanitation systems. Sabin also believed that nursing babies acquired immunity from their mothers. Strongly opposed to Salk's method of using a killed-virus vaccine, Sabin invented an oral vaccine that used the live virus in 1960.

While Salk's work had been far more difficult than some critics said, Sabin and others nonetheless believed that an inactive-virus vaccine was simply not strong enough to give long-term protection. They had good reasons for this attitude: An inactive-virus vaccine for mumps developed in the United States in 1948 had worked—but not very well. People vaccinated with it only stayed immune for about one year.

Meanwhile, polio outbreaks continued to appear, especially in Canada. Antibodies produced by Salk's vaccine only stopped polioviruses from getting into the nervous system. A person receiving Salk's vaccine would usually not develop full-blown polio, but might still carry it in his or her intestine. They could pass the disease on to other people. The problem with Salk's vaccine was that it could not stop polio from spreading.

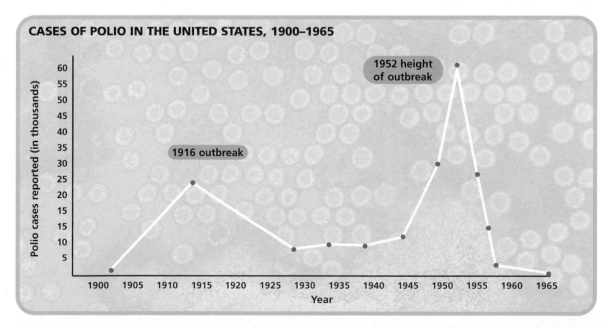

CASES OF POLIO IN THE UNITED STATES, 1900–1965

1952 height of outbreak

1916 outbreak

Polio cases reported (in thousands)

Year

Below: People in every town and city across the United States lined up by the thousands to receive polio vaccinations at dedicated sites. As a result, new cases of polio dropped from nearly 58,000 in 1952 to only 2,500 new cases in 1960. This picture shows an immunization center in Texas in 1962.

Fact

THE VACCINE'S SUCCESS
The Salk and Sabin vaccines had a dramatic effect on polio in the United States. In 1955, nearly 29,000 cases were reported, but in 1960 that number dropped to 2,500 cases. By 1965, only 61 cases were reported. Since then, fewer than 10 cases (usually caused by the vaccine itself) were reported annually. By 1994, polio was considered eradicated in North America.

Above: U.S. president Dwight D. Eisenhower acknowledges Jonas Salk's contribution to the decline of polio with a special award.

SABIN'S VACCINE

Sabin believed that a polio vaccine needed to "trick" the immune system into developing antibodies to fight the polioviruses throughout the body. He was convinced that his polio vaccine would be cheaper, easier to use, and more effective.

Sabin isolated and grew weak versions of each of the three main poliovirus types. These viruses would infect the body—although not seriously—by invading the digestive system. There, the viruses would multiply, but unlike the dangerous forms of polio, would not infect the nervous system. Instead, the viruses would encourage the continued production of antibodies and cause long-term immunity. Weakened forms of the viruses that passed to nonvaccinated people also caused the production of antibodies, which made the new hosts immune as well.

Sabin's oral polio vaccine, or OPV, was swallowed on a lump of sugar or in a spoonful of syrup. It was cheap, so manufacturers and governments liked it, and it was much easier to give to children, which meant doctors, parents, and children liked it, too.

Trials of Sabin's new vaccine started in 1957 in the Netherlands, Sweden, the former Soviet Union, Mexico, Chile, and Japan. Children needed one dose three times in the first two years of life, followed by a booster when they started school. There was no need for further vaccinations.

Even this was not perfect, though. Being "live," Sabin's vaccine can mutate back into a dangerous form. Approximately one in 3.5 million people catch polio from the Sabin vaccine today. By 1964, at least 57 cases of polio leading to paralysis had been caused by the Sabin vaccine in the United States. Also, Sabin's vaccine could not be used on anyone who

was already weak or ill. Even though the virus was weakened, it could give such people full-blown polio. This also meant that anyone working with these sick people, such as doctors or nurses, could not use it either—in case their patients caught polio from them. In the developing world especially, other viruses that live in the gut can prevent the polio vaccine from producing antibodies. These problems highlighted the fact that, even after all the research, poliovirus was still not fully understood. Despite the difficulties, Sabin's vaccine was cheaper, easier to take, and usually more effective than Salk's. By 1962, it was licensed in the United States.

Fact

NEW VACCINATIONS

Now that it was possible to grow viruses in bulk, research could expand in ways previously thought impossible. Polio became part of the series of routine immunzations licensed in 1958 that included DTP, already being given for diphtheria, whooping cough ("pertussis"), and tetanus. Enders' team had shown how viruses could be grown on ordinary living tissue without fear of contamination. In 1954, Enders isolated the measles virus. A measles vaccine was developed by 1960, but it was not made available for the public until 1964. A rubella vaccine was licensed in 1969. The last major epidemic of rubella in the U.S. occurred in 1964, causing damage to 20,000 unborn babies. By 1972, the combined measles-mumps-rubella vaccine, known as MMR, became available. It vaccinates against all three diseases in one dose.

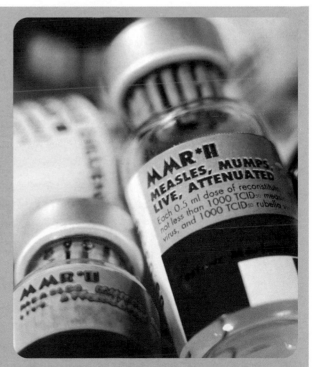

Above: Bottles of the MMR (measles-mumps-rubella) vaccine. Like the polio vaccine, this was at first hailed as a breakthrough. Recently, however, some doctors have suggested that this combined vaccine might cause serious side effects.

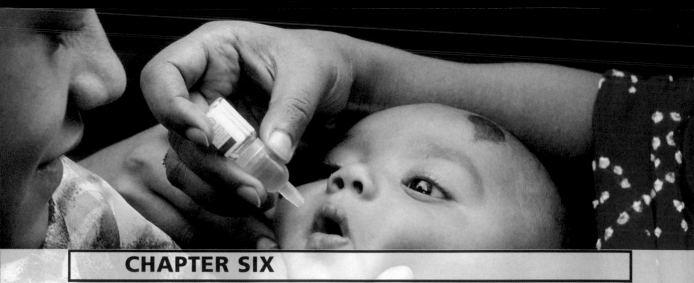

CHAPTER SIX

"The goal of the Global Polio Eradication Initiative is to ensure that no child will ever again know the crippling effects of polio."
WORLD HEALTH ORGANIZATION

Polio Today

Above: *An infant receives the oral polio vaccine.*

Below: *A polio inoculation kit. The inoculation gun forces the vaccine through the skin without the use of a needle, making mass vaccinations much more efficient.*

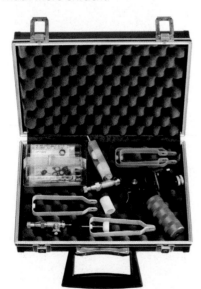

Disease-causing microorganisms are all around, and they can mutate into new forms unaffected by vaccines. Countries with well-established vaccination requirements may still experience disease breakouts. The problems faced by Salk and Sabin when developing their polio vaccines emphasized the difficulties of such efforts. Even now, both the Salk and Sabin vaccines have the potential to cause the disease they are designed to prevent.

THE DECLINE OF POLIO IN THE WEST

In 1959, polio killed a famous English soccer player named Jeff Hall. The high profile of Hall's case reminded people of the dangers of the disease and spurred an increase in the number of polio vaccinations. The subsequent reduction in polio cases created a false sense of security that everyone was safe and that polio was no longer a problem. Within a short time, vaccination numbers dropped off, which again caused an increase in new cases of polio. This

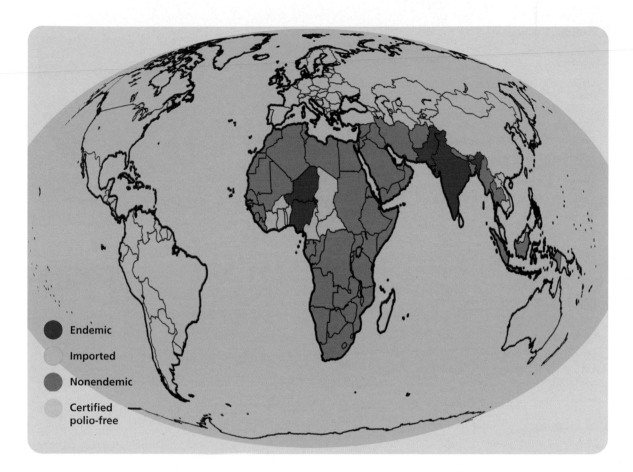

Endemic

Imported

Nonendemic

Certified
polio-free

fluctuation in vaccination levels was reflected in countries across Europe. In the ensuing decades, government sponsored anti-polio campaigns made people realize that eradicating the disease meant everyone must be vaccinated. The United States recorded its last indigenous (naturally occuring) case of polio in 1979.

PLANS FOR A POLIO-FREE WORLD

In 1985, the United Nations Children's Fund (UNICEF) and the World Health Organization (WHO) launched its Universal Childhood Immunization Initiative (UCII), aimed at reducing childhood mortality from polio. Eradicating the disease meant immunizing all children with four doses of polio vaccine before their first birthday. The campaign included National Immunization Days and involved vaccinating of large numbers of children on the same

Above: Polio cases worldwide today. The United States and Europe are polio-free, but polio remains endemic (present in localized areas) in parts of Africa and India.

Fact

THE SALK AND SABIN VACCINES TODAY
Until about the year 2000, Sabin's
oral vaccine, rather than Salk's,
injectable vaccine, was commonly
used around the world. Since it
is a live-virus vaccine, however,
it still causes about seven cases
of polio a year. Researchers are
taking another look at the
advantages and disadvantages of
both types of vaccine. The use
of Salk's killed-virus vaccine
is gaining popularity.

Right: A mother cradles an Indian baby receiving Sabin's oral vaccine. Sabin's vaccine was preferred over Salk's, but because of the small incidence of new polio cases, some experts now say that Salk's vaccine is better after all.

day all around the world. By 1990, the UCII reported achieving its goal of 80 percent childhood immunizations worldwide. China sponsored its first National Immunization Day in 1994—the same year that the International Commission for the Certification of Polio Eradication declared the Americas polio-free.

NEW OUTBREAKS OF POLIO

In 1988, the developing world reported 350,000 cases of polio. By 1990, that number dropped to 116,000; however, accurate figures are nearly impossible because cases of polio in remote areas often go unreported. The live virus in the oral vaccine retains the ability to mutate and cause outbreaks of polio, especially in countries where less than 90 percent of the population gets vaccinated. In the Western Hemisphere, polio broke out in the Dominican Republic in 1999 and Haiti in 2001 because vaccination levels fell below 80 percent of the population.

In China in 2000, a mass-vaccination program followed an outbreak in Qinghai province. In 2002, cases of polio occurred in Africa, in parts of Pakistan, Afghanistan, and India, and in Southeast Asia. A polio outbreak in Nigeria in 2003, linked to contaminated vaccines, later spread to previously polio-free neighboring countries after Muslim clerics convinced citizens that the vaccines were actually contaminated on purpose in a sort of biological terrorist act against Islam. In the public scare that followed, thousands of people refused vaccinations.

The unintentional export of poliovirus to unaffected areas also poses an ever-present threat, particularly in West Africa. Children in these countries are particularly vulnerable: A lack of funds can interrupt immunization campaigns, leaving millions at risk of infection.

In today's era of international travel, anyone carrying a disease can accidentally introduce it to another country. Visitors to affected areas sometimes contract a virus and transport it back to their home countries. An epidemic such as a polio outbreak can thus spread rapidly among nonvaccinated individuals. The main lesson is that worldwide immunity levels for infectious diseases must be maintained.

Fact

MUTATING VIRUSES
New vaccines must be developed regularly for the influenza virus because it mutates continuously. The virus that causes HIV/AIDS by destroying the body's immune system also mutates so quickly that so far, developing a vaccine for it has proved impossible. For the moment, polio vaccines are effective against the three known virus types that cause it. Someday, poliovirus may also mutate into a form that is not affected by the current vaccines.

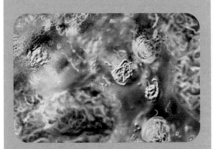

Above: The HIV virus that causes AIDS is a mutating virus. Developing a vaccine for it is very difficult. The virus particles (the green-and-brown spheres, left and top right) attack white blood cells, whose antibodies are ineffective against the virus.

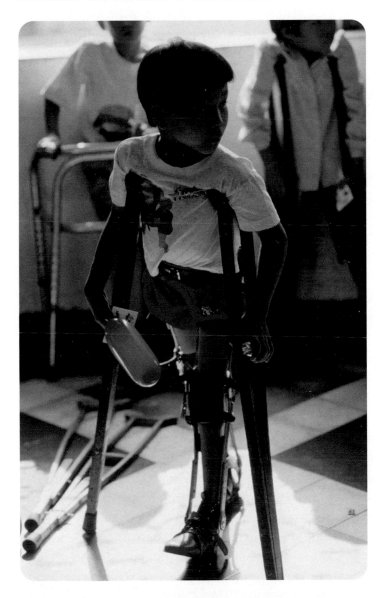

Left: This Vietnamese boy lives in an orphanage for children affected by polio. Many adult polio victims from the 1950s or earlier who recovered from polio as children must now deal with the effects and complications known as post-polio syndrome.

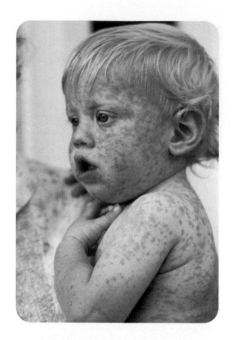

Above: *This young child has measles, an often dangerous disease. Most parents vaccinate their infants and young children against the disease.*

Fact

```
THE DIPHTHERIA VACCINE
By the 1920s, a vaccine
was available for
diphtheria, a disease
that was more common
than polio and which had
a higher death rate. Many
people distrusted the
idea of being vaccinated
at all. The diphtheria
vaccine was tried out in
Britain. Only after news
of its success spread was
it gradually adopted,
with mass vaccinations
beginning in 1941. By the
early 1950s, diphtheria
had almost disappeared.
```

Fears remain that polio could reappear by accident or malicious intent. Poliovirus stocks in laboratories or vaccine-production factories could escape into the general population if a staff member unknowingly became infected and managed to spread the virus. Some people believe that bioterrorists could try to steal the virus or even isolate forms of poliovirus. In 2002, Dr. Eckard Wimmer's research team at State University of New York at Stony Brook announced the creation of an artificial poliovirus from polio's genetic code. The accomplishment not only proved that infectious viruses could be fabricated in laboratories, but also highlighted the need for keeping such information and techniques safe from bioterrorists.

LIVING WITH THE AFTEREFFECTS OF POLIO

An estimated twenty million people worldwide who suffered from polio at its height in the 1940s and 1950s survive today. Some of them spent years in a hospital or at least endured strenuous physical therapy sessions before recovering some mobility. Many of these people, even those who seemed to enjoy a full recovery, now find themselves suffering from the aftereffects of this vicious disease decades later. Their late-onset symptoms, labeled "post-polio syndrome," include muscle weakness, problems breathing or swallowing, muscle pain, and unusual tiredness.

OTHER VIRUSES AND VACCINES

The battle against diseases takes a very long time. Even in the twentieth century, smallpox killed millions of people. In 1967, WHO announced a program to wipe out smallpox. The plan's success depended on organization, money, and worldwide acceptance of vaccination. At least 80 percent (preferably 90 percent) of a population must undergo immunization in order to eradicate a disease; if a lower percentage of the population is vaccinated, a disease remains virulent and contagious among unvaccinated individuals. Achieving that 90 percent immunization level involves organizing and establishing routine vaccination schedules to reach everyone in an area within a short time span, followed by ongoing vaccinations for children and babies.

Health authorities have proof that this plan works: One of the greatest achievements in immunization history came with the announcement in 1980—nearly two hundred years after Edward Jenner's work with cowpox—that smallpox had finally been eradicated.

Still, the science behind vaccinations is relatively new and their success is not always guaranteed. For instance, some parents claim that their children developed intestinal diseases and autism after receiving the measles, mumps, and rubella (MMR) vaccination. Certain researchers believe that giving three vaccinations at once is the problem. Others say that a component of the vaccine itself—unrelated to the viruses—may cause the maladies. Research into the matter continues.

Above: *A British poster promotes immunization as the most effective way to prevent disease. The worldwide success rate of using vaccines against polio proves it is true.*

WHAT DOES THE FUTURE HOLD?

Today, the world sits on the brink of eradicating poliovirus. By the end of 2005, WHO may meet its goal of wiping out the disease forever. It can then turn its attention to battling other deadly medical foes.

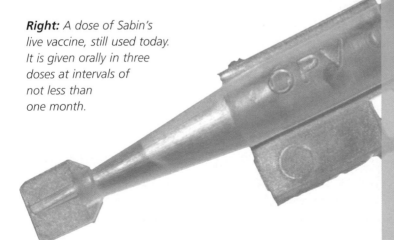

Right: *A dose of Sabin's live vaccine, still used today. It is given orally in three doses at intervals of not less than one month.*

"Never before has commitment and effort been so focused on this final push to rid the world of polio. Not only is the world on the verge of reaching a global health goal—the eradication of polio will also leave behind a legacy of what can be achieved through an extraordinary demonstration of global cooperation."
THE WORLD HEALTH ORGANIZATION, 2004

TIME LINE

1718	Lady Mary Wortley Montagu introduces variolation to England from Turkey
1835	Worksop, Nottinghamshire, England, is first to report a polio epidemic
1853	Dr. Jenner's vaccination against smallpox is made compulsory in England
1909	Dr. Karl Landsteiner discovers that a virus causes polio
1916	First major outbreak of polio in the United States
1931	Scientists discover that polio is caused by more than one type of poliovirus
1938	President Roosevelt creates the National Foundation for Infantile Paralysis
1947	Dr. Jonas Salk heads the polio vaccine research program at the University of Pittsburgh, Pennsylvania; Britain suffers its first major polio outbreak: nearly eight thousand cases are reported
1948	Dr. Isabel Morgan pioneers the use of "killed" poliovirus grown in monkey neural tissue to immunize monkeys
1949	Dr. John F. Enders pioneers the process of growing poliovirus in nonneural tissue cultures
1950	Salk uses the Enders technique to grow poliovirus
1951	Salk's team uses formalin to kill the virus they have grown, experimenting on monkeys successfully to produce immunity
1952	Major polio outbreaks in Denmark and the U.S.; nearly 58,000 U.S. cases of polio are reported; trials of the polio vaccine begin in Pennsylvania
1954	Mass polio vaccine trials in the United States begin in April
1955	Salk announces the success of his vaccine; Albert Sabin begins work on a live-virus vaccine
1961	Polio is reduced in the United States by 95 percent; in Britain, an outbreak in Hull proves that polio still poses a threat
1962	Sabin introduces his live-virus vaccine
1988	The World Health Assembly, the World Health Organization's policy-making branch, votes for a global polio eradication program; 350,000 cases of polio are reported worldwide
1999	Sabin's vaccine is discontinued in the U.S. to prevent further outbreaks
2003	Fewer than seven hundred cases are reported worldwide; the World Health Organization sets a goal of a polio-free world by 2005
2004	A bad batch of polio vaccine in Nigeria, Africa, causes Muslim clerics to urge against vaccination; new cases top 1,000 after spreading to previously disease-free African nations; the British government revives the safer, killed-virus vaccine for a new multivaccine
2005	Polio remains a problem in developing countries throughout Africa; WHO claims Asia will meet polio-free goal by year's end

GLOSSARY

acquired immunity an organism's immune system response to a pathogen that occurs because of the previous introduction of the antigens of that pathogen to the organism.

AIDS (Acquired Immunodeficiency Syndrome) a viral disease that destroys the human immune system, allowing other diseases that would not normally cause problems to become serious illnesses.

alchemy a medieval science that worked to turn base metals into gold and to search for an "elixir" that would prolong human life.

antibody a "fighter cell" of the immune system; produced by white blood cells; it recognizes and attacks invading cells, such as bacteria or viruses.

antigen a protein on the surface of invading cells that provokes an immune response.

antitoxin an antibody that destroys a toxin.

attenuated virus a live, but weakened, virus that is unable to cause disease.

autism a developmental brain disorder that causes communicative and social difficulties.

bacterium a single-celled microorganism capable of independent life.

bioterrorists people who use biological substances to cause harm.

boils inflamed, pussy skin lesions.

booster a vaccine given a certain amount of time after an original dose of vaccine to "boost" its effectiveness against a disease.

cholera an intestinal infection, usually caused by contaminated water or food, that causes severe diarrhea, dehydration, or even death.

cowpox a viral disease of cattle similar to smallpox; once used to inoculate and protect humans against smallpox.

DNA (deoxyribonucleic acid) the nucleic acid that contains the genetic code of an organism.

efficacy effectiveness.

endemic native to a certain area or population.

epidemic a (usually) sudden breakout of disease that infects a significant proportion of the population.

formalin a 37 percent-diluted solution of formaldehyde, a powerful disinfectant and preservative; can be used in vaccines.

gene a segment of DNA that carries information that determines an organism's characteristics.

genetic code the sequence of genetic material that holds the key to the development, behavior, and physiology of an organism.

HIV (Human Immunodeficiency Virus) a virus that disables the human immune system, making it incapable of fighting diseases.

immune system a collection of cells and proteins that recognize and protect the body from harmful microorganisms.

immunization the introduction of foreign substances into an organism with the intent of causing an immune system reaction that prevents or lessens the effects of disease.

incubation period a symptom-free time span that includes a host's initial exposure to an infective agent and during which the host is capable of spreading that infectious agent to others, but before full-blown symptoms develop in the host.

indigenous naturally occurring.

inoculation the introduction of a pathogen into the body in order to stimulate an immune system response.

IPV (Inactive Polio Vaccine) a "killed" polio vaccine made from inactive poliovirus; developed by Jonas Salk and his team.

iron lung a horizontal metal cylinder used by polio patients unable to breathe on their own. As a polio victim lies inside the cylinder, the iron lung varies air pressure between high and low, which moves the person's diaphragm up and down in order to expand and contract the lungs, as in normal breathing.

microorganism any organism visible only under a microscope.

OPV (Oral Polio Vaccine) a live but attenuated, or weakened, polio vaccine; developed by Albert Sabin as an alternative to Salk's vaccine.

pathogen any microorganism, such as a bacterium or virus, that causes disease.

penicillin one of a group of antibacterial drugs called antibiotics. Penicillin works by killing disease-causing bacteria.

plague a highly infectious and often deadly disease that caused a high fever and internal and external pustules.

poliomyelitis the full name for polio, a highly contagious "filth" disease that affects the motor nerve cells; can cause muscle weakness, paralysis, and death; some victims recover full use of their limbs while others remain disabled; from the Greek words *polios*, meaning "gray," and *muelos*, meaning "marrow," referring to the gray coloring of the spinal cord.

RNA (ribonucleic acid) an acid that uses information from DNA to produce cell proteins. In viruses, RNA works as a kind of ultrasimple DNA that contains the genetic information.

smallpox a very contagious viral disease, causing high fever and a rash.

symptom a sign of illness; an indicator that the body is not working properly.

toxin a naturally occurring poisonous substance that can cause disease.

transmission the passing of diseases from one cell or organism to another.

typhoid fever a dangerous infection caused by the bacterium *Salmonella typhi*; symptoms include high fever and diarrhea; can be deadly; spreads through contaminated food or water.

vaccination the process of administering a vaccine as a precaution against contracting a disease.

vaccine a virus-containing solution, prepared for the purpose of inoculating humans and other animals, that causes the immune system to react to a specific disease-causing organism by producing antibodies that fight and kill the invading organism.

virus a one-celled microorganism consisting of genetic material in a protein "coat." A virus cannot cannot live on its own and must invade another organism to survive and reproduce.

white blood cells immune system cells in the blood that recognize and destroy harmful bacteria, viruses, and fungi.

FURTHER INFORMATION

BOOKS

Bankston, John. *Jonas Salk and the Polio Vaccine. Unlocking the Secrets of Science* (series). Mitchell Lane Publishers (2001).

Barter, James. *The Importance of Jonas Salk.* Lucent (2003).

Brunelle, Lynn and Mark Gave. *Viruses. Discovery Channel School Science* (series). Gareth Stevens Publishing (2003).

Goldstein, Natalie. *Viruses. Germs! The Library of Disease-Causing Organisms* (series). Rosen (2004).

Hantula, Richard. *Jonas Salk. Trailblazers of the Modern World* (series). Gareth Stevens Publishing (2004).

Hecht, Alan. *Polio. Deadly Diseases and Epidemics* (series). Chelsea House (2003).

McPherson, Stephanie Sammartino. *Jonas Salk: Conquering Polio. Lerner Biographies* (series). Lerner (2001).

Monroe, Judy. *Influenza and Other Viruses. Perspectives on Disease and Illness* (series). Capstone (2001).

Routh, Kristina. *AIDS. 21st Century Issues* (series). Gareth Stevens Publishing (2004).

Thomas, Peggy. *Bacteria and Viruses. Lucent Library of Science and Technology* (series). Lucent (2004).

Tocci, Salvatore. *Jonas Salk: Creator of the Polio Vaccine. Great Minds of Science* (series). Enslow (2003).

WEB SITES

www.answers.com/topic/jonas-salk
Read a short biography of Jonas Salk and explore a series of related links.

www.marchofdimes.com
Visit the home page of the March of Dimes.

www.pbs.org/wgbh/aso/ontheedge/polio/
Take a comic-strip odyssey to learn the amazing tale of Dr. Salk's vaccine.

www.polioeradication.org/history.asp
Follow a time line outlining the history of polio.

www.who.int/mediacentre/factsheets/fs114/en/
Discover what's happening in the international fight to eradicate polio.

INDEX